ADVENT

Zachary Collins

ADVENT

Zachary Collins

ADVENT
Copyright©2019 Zachary Collins
All Rights Reserved
Published by Unsolicited Press
Printed in the United States of America.
First Edition 2019.

All rights reserved. Printed in the United States of America. No part of this book may be used or reproduced in any manner whatsoever without written permission except in the case of brief quotations embodied in critical articles or reviews.

Attention schools and businesses: for discounted copies on large orders, please contact the publisher directly. Books are brought to the trade by Ingram.

For information contact:
Unsolicited Press
Portland, Oregon
www.unsolicitedpress.com
orders@unsolicitedpress.com
619-354-8005

Cover Design: Kathryn Gerhardt
Editor: S.R. Stewart
ISBN: 978-1-950730-62-9

TABLE OF CONTENTS

Saturday Morning	9
The Outsider's Insight	10
Toy Cups	11
Dad Jokes	12
When You Stood	13
Olive Branch	14
Advent	15
Hemangioma	17
Thanksgiving Blessing, 2016	18
Sometimes	19
First Date	21
Cartographers of Skin and Sky	22
Now and Then	23
The Stowaway Promise	24
Midwest Coast	25
Tearfall	26
Movie Night	27
Fixed	28
The Price or Iscariot, Forgive Me	29
Jesus from the Trailer Park	30
Prodigal	31

Autumn Leaves, Late December   32
I'm Sorry   33
July   34
Get It   35

SATURDAY MORNING

The sun rises,
Wiggles you awake

Your mom inhales the day like
It's going to end, and it will
But not before wearing you like her favorite dress
And dancing on the hours in between
Champagne at the last wedding of the summer

I measure minutes in the sky
Counting the daylight's ribbons as
They unwind themselves flat on the floor
Listening to you sing from
An empty Colosseum

THE OUTSIDER'S INSIGHT

Your eyes tell me who I am.
When you sleep, when she sleeps,
I feel like nobody to anybody special.

A smile in the morning and a kiss goodnight,
I am a lucky king,
But in the eyes staring back
From black coffee in a mug I bought myself,
I'm nobody to anybody special.

TOY CUPS

Three little cups
That fit like Russian dolls
Into one another

Your 8-month mind—
Sprouting waves of wildflowers,
A meadow in a moment

Your hands move like an artisan's
Putting together pieces of the sun
The cups are worlds colliding

A universe scattered out on the
Belly-breathing workbench
A father watching his girl condense

Time and space into three toy cups
A diamond made and tossed away
In pursuit of something still more precious

DAD JOKES

A guy walks into a bar
Says *Damn, that hurts*
He's not talking about the bar though

I ask and he tells me he hates his job
And his relationship
Is going nowhere; he knows he won't
Have the family
He's spent too much time trying to build
He asks if I know what that feels like
But he isn't looking for an answer

Instead I order a round and chat about
The World Series
My wife and daughter
He's spilling salted memories into his beer
They're splashing on the table, falling on my shoes
So I say *Hey* with an anticipated grin
I got a good one

WHEN YOU STOOD

When you stood for the first time,
You stood hundreds of feet tall –
Into the infinite sky
Of everything possible.
Your feet tickled the grey-green carpeting
And turned the Earth
A little quicker.

When you stood, your eyes filled with a sea
Of adventure,
Waves and winds carrying dreams boundless.
Your lips curled like pages of an old book
Begging to be read.

You touched land and sea and sky
All at once,
And in the smallest breath you blew
A word with no letters,
Only the tiny sound of a lifelong triumph.

Your mighty hands grasped firmly to the
Hand-me-down furniture –
To the future upon which you mounted
Your endeavor,
But your tides changed, and a world unready
For you pulled so you might again stand
And turn the Earth
A little quicker.

OLIVE BRANCH

The best sound in the world:
You laughed at me first.

Nana and Papa say,
No one makes you laugh like Daddy,
I sometimes feel guilty it's true;
You always laugh at me first.

Doves fly high overhead,
White feathers darkened in silhouette.

But when you laugh,
You fill the house and flood the streets.
Before we run for the ark, and peer through
Sweaty windows
Gaping at the sky,

Before a single raindrop falls from
A dark cloud on a white wing,
You laughed at me first.

ADVENT

On the evening you were born, I remember snow.
That might have been the day before,
I remember how it felt like spring when
We brought you home
But before you came, there was snow.

I remember your mom, who
Recently had a nightmare
Because I joked that my sore tooth was haunted,
Fearless for the first time on the evening
You were born.
I remember being exhilarated
And terrified
And helpless
And hiding it all from her while she brought
The skies of Earth to you. And you to me.

I remember your first breath brought about
My first breath,
Your first cry – my first cry.

Your mom lied back, unaffected
By the river of doctors and nurses
Streaming to and from her,
And watched, content, two faces
She had never seen before
Meet for the first time. Maybe she was
Just exhausted,

Or maybe it was the epidural. Probably,
It was a convergence of everything,
But that's what I remember.

HEMANGIOMA

That spot on your head, it worried us for a while
It grew with you and ruptured and bled

You cried
We called the doctor to
Admit what we didn't know

Hemangioma
We could pronounce it by now

She's got a strawberry
She's got a stork-bite

She's got a benign vascular tumor
Comprised of a surplus of endothelial cells
Lining a cluster of blood vessels which
Result in a reddish-pink pigmentation

Don't stare at my kid
She's perfect

THANKSGIVING BLESSING, 2016

I only pray sometimes
Perhaps not as often as I should
But sometimes is enough
To say thank you

There are always wants
And evermore needs
But for the family I have
Infinitely and profoundly
I say thank you

For the family you will have
The fun and joy
The lessons and tears
The responsibility you have
Given me to be better than
I am
For you

And the clarity to know
I am happy
I pray simply to say
Thank you

SOMETIMES

You should know: I try to be a good man.

I bring flowers, on occasion,
Home to your mom
to show her that every time
I see something beautiful,
I think of her.

Sometimes I think flowers and forget.
Sometimes I'm too tired.
I try to be a good man.

I have so much fun at family parties,
I eat more appetizers than meal, I drink Heineken,
and laugh while I
Pretend that I can sympathize with the
Stories of hijinks the Uncles tell of their youths.

Sometimes we double-book on those weekends.
Sometimes I just want to be alone,
But I try to be a good man.

I love rocking you to sleep, one forearm
Tucked behind your knees, and the other hand
Drumming a rhythm onto your slumped back
While you hum yourself to sleep.

Sometimes my arm falls asleep before you.

Sometimes I have other things to do.
Still, I need you to know
I try to be a good man.

FIRST DATE

I never should have had one in the first place.
Thank God she was bored before that.

I planned it for days, and
It was still cheesy and awkward.

I am proud of the pennies though,
A roll of pennies and a fountain at the mall;
We cast wishes into water, but they landed
Where our smiles were more real now.
I think that's when she made her decision.

I still can't believe
I baked brownies,
And she never ate them.

CARTOGRAPHERS OF SKIN AND SKY

With mosquitoes on our backs and
Stars on our tongues,
We swung our feet from the port of our future
Mapped in fireworks and wine.

Cold water raised bumps we tried
To press down for each other.

A bat flew out from my truck and
Threatened us with a memory
Screeched into the night.

We lay down, laughing in the street,
Happy for the rest of time.

NOW AND THEN

Seconds on my watch slide off like
Drops from the leaky faucet in our bathtub I never
Make time to stop and fix

It was a gift she gave me for our wedding

Rose gold hands summersault in white sunlight
Knowing they will find their way
Home again before dark

The hands never reach behind themselves
Interested in collecting seconds
On their fingers like
Empty beer bottles from a birthday party or
Photos rearranged in an
Album that hasn't been opened
Since it was arranged the first time

Our hands should be those hands
Dollar-store butterfly nets I had as a kid
Chasing each other with laughter stuck in our teeth

THE STOWAWAY PROMISE

My eyes: red from chlorine and rum
Chase her dancing down sloping streets
To *chak-chak* raining *Kwadril* and clouds thundering
Calypso
Flood-water fills her flip-flops,
Splashes as high as her smile

My tongue: struggles to say *Hees salop!* through
Mango and saltwater while

My ears: hear golf-course landscapers and piano
players beg through laughter –
don't tell our bosses we taught you to curse

My nose: tickled awake by her hair
Scents of sunscreen, black tea, hotel linen
Her skin like warm sugar

My hands: her hands
New rings crash into freckle-stained shoulders

Arms like albatross wings
Tracing horizon lines across the curve of the swell
And you wading just below the surface
Waiting to see the sunrise

MIDWEST COAST

Messages in a bottle –
We don't live near the sea,
But we made do.

Inscribing onto paper the
Bulges growing in our chests,
We filled our pages with letters
Carved too carefully for the water.

So we kept the messages for ourselves and
Bottled up the sea.

TEARFALL

Thorns of silver dig into the lips of my eyes,
Never willing to fall over the edge, into the cold.
So few have seen them more than twice.

A quiet slumber and a loud goodbye
All in the same year,
And my father's voice begging
Through a bad connection
For what to do next.
More sandbags on the levee.

The silver softens when we're on the couch,
Together yet quiet,
And the thorns thin and break.
She alone has permission to
Bathe in a moonlit Jordan
Without realizing that even the
Sun had looked away.

MOVIE NIGHT

As we left the movie,
I can't recall which one,
An old jazzy song played overhead
In the theatre lobby.

It was the last show for the night.
Teenage ushers swept popcorn and paper cups
Into rolling bins, their black bowties and flat-caps
Bitterly betraying the idols of cool.

I stopped on the way out, taking
Her hand in mine, and we danced to
an unnamed tune of fading horns and
Garbage bags
Flapped open to make a point, then
Hastily inserted into cans.

A girl counted coins on the glass-top counter:

Sounds that haunted our silent heels on a
Stained mosaic carpet which
Had just been vacuumed.

FIXED

There were nights when I was a younger man
trying so hard to become *a man*—
I sipped midnight bourbon from a coffee mug,
read Steinbeck while my spirit corroded
In another place:

East of Eden,
West of civilization

Before your mother swelled with you, before
You conspired in the stars to save me,
I was stuck in the quick-dry
Cement of my future

Getting harder by the minute. Cheap powdered
cement
Mixed in a bucket with a stick by an
Unlicensed workman
Trying to figure it out from the back of his
Pick-up.

THE PRICE OR ISCARIOT, FORGIVE ME

Thirty pieces of silver;
Thirty coins that honor a promise to
Kiss unwashed feet goodnight
As they race their benefactor to the ground.

One kiss;
One tree in an empty field shutters
And can't tell one quiet crack from another.

Forever;
Forgiveness takes its time, careful
To untie a taut rope weighed heavy by
Thirty pieces of silver.

JESUS FROM THE TRAILER PARK

There was this dude in his thirties,
Looked like Jesus –
Sandals, long hair, long stares
From eyes dark as caves
Wherein he spent three sleepless days
Shrouded in silken nightmares –

He wandered into
A backyard bonfire between neighbors
One night at the trailer park.

Parents were cautious around him;
He would often stop and chat with
Kids, namely girls, as they'd walk
Home from the school bus.

He crept past the neighbors on this night –
Booze-bloated parents and their sun-stained kids
Begging for attention.

Drunken fathers of girls in the park,
Mine was one,
Watched him linger for a moment,
Then wiped the foamy courage from
Their weekend whiskers.

This dude who couldn't save himself shouted
Salvation! as our dads lets the devil hold their beers

PRODIGAL

I raised my sister;
Of course not in such a way as to have paid
For her upbringing, but I did feed her every day
When we got home from school
And brought her outside with me to play –
To learn what our lives could be.

Still, she clung to the adults –
The ones I wanted to cling to,
And each time, I felt like a failure,
Like I never opened her eyes
Or loved her correctly.

I'm only ten I rationalized,
But it didn't make me feel better
Sitting at the dining-room table watching,
Up close and from afar,
My family love each other
Over a dried-out beef roast and
Lumpy mashed potatoes.

Dinner rarely smelled good,
But I needed to eat,
And I was hungry nonetheless.

AUTUMN LEAVES, LATE DECEMBER

The autumn leaves in our backyard
no longer freshly browned and delicately
Cast off by October trees in the setting sun.
They are not crisp and do not crunch when
The dog chases his ball past the half-dressed ash.

It's late December now, and all the
Leaves are still-born: sodden and limp.
The warmth
Of red and orange and yellow has burned
And flitted
And died
And now the sorry leaves lie still,

Like a body waiting for another snow
To hide its nakedness from
The family who watches with disappointment
Through a sliding glass door while
The dog takes too long to piss.

I'M SORRY

He shaved his mustache once
A face fresh and proud for a moment

He looked different

We noted it immediately
Wife and daughter and son
Laughed at strangeness on
A man we knew better than that

He started to look the same again

Before he sat silent on the couch and lit a cigarette
He had already begun growing it back

JULY

I used to count the seconds between the flashes
Of lightning and the rumble of thunder
To see how many miles away
From me the storm was —
Something my mom told me,
Which I knew wasn't true.

My parents glorified thunderstorms;
They taught my sister and me to love them.
We would go out onto the patio of our tiny
Third-story apartment,
Or stand bare-foot in the muddied
Grass of the communal backyard
And watch lightning crack the sky in half,
Applaud the night for her loudest bursts of thunder.

In hindsight, it was a clever way
To teach us not to fear the chaos that our lives —
Their lives —
Held as norm.

It was their lesson in courage.
It was their apology.

And we learned on the wind-cut nights
In the July heat
To stand solid in the sinking mud
And to never blink the rain from our eyes.

GET IT

No arrangement of words, no matter
How well punctuated or imaginative, can
Tell the story of a man.

His pen is not the sword that guts
The dragons in his past, nor is it the
Sabre in the hands of a king – adherents
Prostrate in the dirt before him.

No. The pen is merely a syringe
Of the man who needs to get right.
Inject himself and you with ink like fever
Dreams scorched into memory,
Shrouded in the smoke of what he felt.

Now you get it.
How does it feel?

ABOUT THE AUTHOR

Zac Collins is a freelance writer and high school English teacher from the south suburbs of Chicago whose students acclaim him as "not the worst, I guess". He is an avid consumer of affordable wine, an aspiring contestant (and preferably winner) of Food Network's *Chopped*, and deeply troubled by his inability to 'pull off' skinny jeans.

Collins and his wife recently welcomed their second daughter, a much-anticipated sister for their eldest daughter, to whom his first collection is written. He and his family currently reside in the suburbs of Chicago in home they swear they just cleaned not too long ago.

ABOUT THE PRESS

Unsolicited Press is nestled in the hills of Portland, Oregon. The press produces stellar works of poetry, fiction, and nonfiction.

Learn more at www.unsolicitedpress.com.

www.ingramcontent.com/pod-product-compliance
Lightning Source LLC
Chambersburg PA
CBHW030135100526
44591CB00009B/677